D1715769

How to Analyze the Works of

J.K. ROWLING

by Victoria Peterson-Hilleque

ABDO
Publishing Company

Essential Critiques

How to Analyze the Works of

J.K. ROWLING

by Victoria Peterson-Hilleque

Content Consultant: Benjamin J. Robertson, instructor,
Department of English, University of Colorado at Boulder

Credits

Published by ABDO Publishing Company, 8000 West 78th Street, Edina, Minnesota 55439. Copyright © 2012 by Abdo Consulting Group, Inc. International copyrights reserved in all countries. No part of this book may be reproduced in any form without written permission from the publisher. The Essential Library™ is a trademark and logo of ABDO Publishing Company.

Printed in the United States of America,
North Mankato, Minnesota
062011
092011

 THIS BOOK CONTAINS AT LEAST 10% RECYCLED MATERIALS.

Editor: Amy Van Zee
Copy Editor: Sarah Beckman
Interior Design and Production: Christa Schneider
Cover Design: Marie Tupy

Library of Congress Cataloging-in-Publication Data
Peterson-Hilleque, Victoria, 1971-
  How to analyze the works of J. K. Rowling / by Victoria Peterson-Hilleque.
    p. cm. -- (Essential critiques)
  Includes bibliographical references and index.
  ISBN 978-1-61783-093-8
  1. Rowling, J. K.--Criticism and interpretation--Juvenile literature. 2. Potter,
Harry (Fictitious character)--Juvenile literature. I. Title.

  PR6068.O93Z823 2011
  823'.914--dc22

                              2011006303

Table of Contents

Chapter

1

Introduction to Critiques

What Is Critical Theory?

What do you usually do when you read a book? You probably absorb the specific language style of the book. You learn about the characters as they are developed through thoughts, dialogue, and other interactions. You may like or dislike a character more than others. You might be drawn in by the plot of the book, eager to find out what happens at the end. Yet these are only a few of many possible ways of understanding and appreciating a book. What if you are interested in delving more deeply? You might want to learn more about the author and how his or her personal background is reflected in the book. Or you might want to examine what the book says about society—how it depicts the roles of women and

minorities, for example. If so, you have entered the realm of critical theory.

Critical theory helps you learn how various works of art, literature, music, theater, film, and other endeavors either support or challenge the way society behaves. Critical theory is the evaluation and interpretation of a work using different philosophies, or schools of thought. Critical theory can be used to understand all types of cultural productions.

There are many different critical theories. If you are analyzing literature, each theory asks you to look at the work from a different perspective. Some theories address social issues, while others focus on the writer's life or the time period in which the book was written or set. For example, the critical theory that asks how an author's life affected the work is called biographical criticism. Other common schools of criticism include historical criticism, feminist criticism, psychological criticism, and New Criticism, which examines a work solely within the context of the work itself.

What Is the Purpose of Critical Theory?

Critical theory can open your mind to new ways of thinking. It can help you evaluate a book from a new perspective, directing your attention to issues and messages you may not otherwise recognize in a work. For example, applying feminist criticism to a book may make you aware of female stereotypes perpetuated in the work. Applying a critical theory to a book helps you learn about the person who created it or the society that enjoyed it. You can also explore how the work is perceived by current cultures.

How Do You Apply Critical Theory?

You conduct a critique when you use a critical theory to examine and question a work. The theory you choose is a lens through which you can view the work, or a springboard for asking questions about the work. Applying a critical theory helps you think critically about the work. You are free to question the work and make an assertion about it. If you choose to examine a book using biographical theory, for example, you want to know how the author's personal background or education inspired or shaped the work. You could explore why the author was drawn to the story. For instance, are there any parallels between a particular character's life and the author's life?

Forming a Thesis

Ask your question and find answers in the work or other related materials. Then you can create a thesis. The thesis is the key point in your critique. It is your argument about the work based on the tenets, or beliefs, of the theory you are using. For example, if you are using biographical theory to ask how the author's life inspired the work, your thesis could be worded as follows: Writer Teng Xiong, raised in refugee camps in Southeast

How to Make a Thesis Statement

In a critique, a thesis statement typically appears at the end of the introductory paragraph. It is usually only one sentence long and states the author's main idea.

Asia, drew upon her experiences to write the novel *No Home for Me*.

Providing Evidence

Once you have formed a thesis, you must provide evidence to support it. Evidence might take the form of examples and quotations from the work itself—such as dialogue from a character. Articles about the book or personal interviews with the author might also support your ideas. You may wish to address what other critics have written about the work. Quotes from these individuals may help support your claim. If you find any quotes or examples that contradict your thesis, you will need to create an argument against them. For instance: Many critics have pointed to the protagonist of *No Home for Me* as a powerless victim of circumstances. However, in the chapter "My Destiny," she is clearly depicted as someone who seeks to shape her own future.

How to Support
a Thesis Statement

A critique should include several arguments. Arguments support a thesis claim. An argument is one or two sentences long and is supported by evidence from the work being discussed.

Organize the arguments into paragraphs. These paragraphs make up the body of the critique.

In This Book

In this book, you will read summaries of famous books by writer J. K. Rowling, each followed by a critique. Each critique will use one theory and apply it to one work. Critical thinking sections will give you a chance to consider other theses and questions about the work. Did you agree with the author's application of the theory? What other questions are raised by the thesis and its arguments? You can also find out what other critics think about each particular book. Then, in the You Critique It section in the final pages of this book, you will have an opportunity to create your own critique.

Look for the Guides

Throughout the chapters that analyze the works, thesis statements have been highlighted. The box next to the thesis helps explain what questions are being raised about the work. Supporting arguments have been underlined. The boxes next to the arguments help explain how these points support the thesis. Look for these guides throughout each critique.

Author J. K. Rowling

2

A Closer Look at J. K. Rowling

Joanne Rowling was born on July 31, 1965, in Chipping Sodbury, England, to Peter and Anne Rowling. She spent most of her childhood in the country. She lived in the town of Tutshill on the border of England and Wales. She loved reading and being read to. Influenced by author and illustrator Richard Scarry, she wrote her first story at a young age about a rabbit sick with the measles.

As a teenager, Joanne loved English and her English teacher, Miss Shepherd. Joanne also became fluent in German and French. Also during her teenage years, Joanne's mother was diagnosed with a severe form of multiple sclerosis.

Joanne graduated from Wyedean Comprehensive Secondary School in 1983 and went on to the University of Exeter in Devon,

England. She studied French and classic literature. She longed to study English, but her parents thought languages would be a more practical route for finding a job. She graduated in 1986, and her aspiration to be a writer was kept secret.

Love, Marriage, and Work

After graduating from college, Rowling worked as a secretary and then for Amnesty International. During breaks and in the evenings, she devoted her attention to writing. During that time, she finished two novels that she never sent for publication because she did not believe they were good enough.

The character of Harry Potter first entered Rowling's mind on a train ride from Manchester to London in 1990. She spent the next 17 years plotting and writing the seven-book series. But first, she had to write the original and find a publisher.

Six months after beginning to write the original book, Rowling's mother died of complications related to multiple sclerosis. Rowling never mentioned her writing project to her mother and would deeply regret keeping her aspirations secret. For Rowling, life after the death of her mother was extremely difficult. To escape, she took a job teaching English in Porto, Portugal. She taught in the evenings and wrote during the day. She fell in love and married Jorge Arantes in 1992. Their daughter, Jessica, was born the following year. When Rowling's marriage to Arantes deteriorated, she and Jessica moved to Scotland to be near Rowling's sister, Diana. Rowling brought three chapters of her Harry Potter novel with her.

Trying to support herself and her daughter as a single parent was not easy. She needed government subsidies to make ends meet. She would write in cafés, while Jessica napped in her baby carriage. Rowling managed to finish the book before joining a teacher certification program in 1995. By that year, her divorce was finalized.

Harry Potter Takes Off

The Christopher Little Literary Agency accepted the book and agreed to help Rowling look for a publisher. Rowling needed to revise the book as well as her name because her agent feared boys would be turned off by a female writer. She took her grandmother's name Kathleen for a middle name to become J. K. Rowling.

After many rejections, a small publishing house, Bloomsbury, bought the rights to print the book in Great Britain in 1996. It was titled *Harry Potter and the Philosopher's Stone*. Because the book did surprisingly well in Britain, the next year, Scholastic bought the rights to print the book in the United States for a lucrative sum. In the United States, it was titled *Harry Potter and the Sorcerer's Stone*. However, Rowling was struggling to write the second Harry Potter book because she was fearful it would not live up to expectations. While she finished it on time for her deadline, she took it back for revisions for six weeks afterward.

The publicity surrounding Rowling and her work overwhelmed her. She did not enjoy the way her history of being a single mother was romanticized. She enjoyed connecting with her fans, but she found the attention from the press disruptive to her personal life. Her fame became an ongoing struggle that lingered throughout the process of writing the series.

Meanwhile, *Harry Potter and the Sorcerer's Stone* was on the best-seller list, and *Harry Potter and the Chamber of Secrets* followed shortly after in Britain in 1998 and in the United States in 1999.

Rowling accepted an honorary degree from the University of Edinburgh in 2004.

The announcement of a movie based on *Harry Potter and the Sorcerer's Stone* in 1998 increased interest in the books and their author. Rowling published *Harry Potter and the Prisoner of Azkaban* in 1999 and *Harry Potter and the Goblet of Fire* in 2000.

All four of the Harry Potter books received an array of different awards such as the British Book Awards Children's Book of the Year, British Book Awards Author of the Year, the Bram Stoker Award, and the Whitbread Children's Book of the Year Award.

Criticism and controversy surrounded the books. Religious conservatives often accused them of promoting the occult. Rowling's response has been to invite dialogue about the matter. She especially criticizes those who want to censor the books without reading them.

Rowling and her husband, Neil Murray, attended the premiere of the film version of *Harry Potter and the Order of the Phoenix* in London in 2007.

Finishing the Series

In the midst of writing, Rowling met and fell in love with Neil Murray, who worked as a physician. They married in 2001. The publications of the next two Harry Potter books coincided with the birth of children. *Harry Potter and the Order of the Phoenix* was preceded by a few months by the birth of Rowling's second child, David, in 2003. Rowling's third child, Mackenzie, preceded *Harry Potter and the Half-Blood Prince* by six months in 2005. Two years later, the final installment, *Harry Potter and the Deathly Hallows,* was finished. Harry Potter movies followed the publications of the books at a quick pace and made billions at the box office. Saying good-bye to writing the Harry Potter series was bittersweet for Rowling. As of 2011, Rowling was working on new writing projects.

Essential Critiques

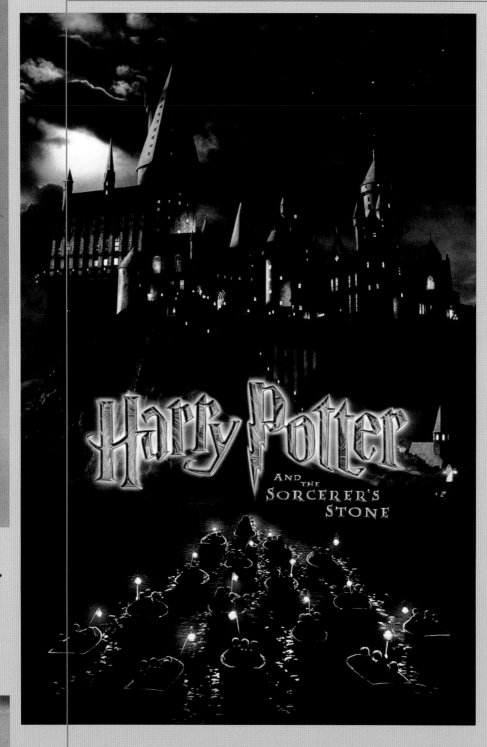

The film version of *Harry Potter and the Sorcerer's Stone* was released in fall 2001.

Chapter 3

An Overview of *Harry Potter and the Sorcerer's Stone*

The story begins with Petunia and Vernon Dursley, who are not happy about raising their nephew, Harry Potter. The Dursleys are Muggles—non-wizards—and are mortified at the thought of raising the child of a witch and a wizard. The Dark wizard Lord Voldemort killed Harry's parents, but infant Harry miraculously survived with a lightning-bolt-shaped scar on his forehead. Voldemort disappeared after the murders, causing much joy in the wizard community and an interest in Harry Potter.

Harry grows up mistreated by the Dursleys and their son, Dudley. Harry notices that strange things happen when he is afraid or angry, but he does not know his history until a letter is delivered inviting him to attend Hogwarts School of Witchcraft and Wizardry.

The Hogwarts Express train takes Harry and his fellow classmates to school. On the train, he meets the people who will become his best friends: Ron Weasley and Hermione Granger. These friendships make him an enemy of Draco Malfoy, who dislikes people who are not pureblood wizards (such as Hermione) and those who defend them (such as Ron's father). Once the students arrive at Hogwarts, they are sorted into four different houses: Slytherin, Gryffindor, Hufflepuff, and Ravenclaw. Harry, Hermione, and Ron are in Gryffindor.

Although new to the wizard world, Harry has old grudges to deal with at Hogwarts. Professor Snape's hatred for Harry is evident within the first few moments in his Potions class. Eventually, Harry, Ron, and Hermione begin to suspect him of something much worse than bullying students. They begin to unravel the mystery of the Sorcerer's Stone.

While out of bed after hours, Harry and his friends sneak into a corridor that has been forbidden to students. They encounter a huge three-headed dog, which they believe to be guarding a package that Harry saw Hagrid, the Hogwarts gamekeeper, withdraw from the bank before school began.

After a troll is let into the school, Harry and Ron begin to wonder if the troll was a diversion. Snape's leg injury—possibly the work of the three-headed dog—leads them to suspect that Snape tried to get at the guarded item.

Hagrid is a former Hogwarts student who is employed by the school. He befriends Harry, Ron, and Hermione.

Quidditch and Magical Gifts

Harry joins the Gryffindor Quidditch team. In this magical sport, players fly on broomsticks. During his first match, Harry's broom acts strangely. Hermione sees Snape whispering while staring at Harry, so she sets Snape's robes on fire to prevent him from cursing the broom. Harry begins to fly normally again and wins the game by swallowing the snitch, a special flying ball.

When Harry, Ron, and Hermione tell Hagrid of their suspicions about Snape, he denies the suspicions but inadvertently gives them a clue, saying the guarded item relates to Nicolas Flamel. They link this with the fact that there was an attempted robbery on the vault Hagrid emptied at the bank.

For Christmas, Harry receives an Invisibility Cloak that once belonged to his father. Using it after hours to research Nicolas Flamel, he accidentally encounters the Mirror of Erised. The reflection shows him standing with his parents and relatives. Harry dreams of the mirror and often sneaks away to stare into it until Dumbledore, the headmaster, tells him it will be moved. Finally, a collector's card from a Chocolate Frog explains that Nicolas Flamel was known for making the Sorcerer's Stone—an object that produces the Elixir of Life and offers eternal life to the bearer.

When Harry sees Snape threatening his Defense Against the Dark Arts teacher, Professor Quirrell,

Harry forms the belief that Snape wants the Sorcerer's Stone and is bullying Quirrell to help him get past the guard dog. Hagrid tells them the teachers at Hogwarts developed enchantments to guard the precious stone.

Hogwarts students gather by house for meals in the Great Hall.

Helping Hagrid smuggle an illegal dragon away from Hogwarts causes Ron, Harry, and Hermione to lose many points for their house and earns them detention in the Forbidden Forest. The centaurs and other creatures that live in the forest are nothing compared to the creature they find feasting on unicorn blood. The sight causes searing pain in Harry's scar. The centaur Firenze tells Harry that unicorn blood will keep someone alive, but the person's life will be cursed. Firenze suggests Voldemort is keeping himself alive with unicorn blood until he can steal the Sorcerer's Stone.

The pieces of the mystery begin to fall into place when Harry, Ron, and Hermione discover that Hagrid told a stranger that the guard dog will fall asleep if music is played. They know that whoever is trying to steal the Sorcerer's Stone has enough information to obtain it. Harry, Hermione, and Ron try to tell Dumbledore, but he has left Hogwarts.

Finding the Sorcerer's Stone

Ron, Hermione, and Harry realize if Voldemort returns to power, life as they know it will be finished. They go after the Sorcerer's Stone. After lulling the guard dog to sleep, the three friends burn their way out of a treacherous plant called a Devil's Snare, play a life-size game of Wizard's chess, and solve a logic puzzle. But it is Harry who must face the last test alone. He is surprised to discover Professor Quirrell standing in front of the Mirror of Erised. Quirrell reveals that he has been trying to get the Sorcerer's Stone. Their conversation reveals that Quirrell let the troll into the school and enchanted Harry's broom at the Quidditch game—Snape was muttering incantations to stop him. Quirrell did all of this while serving Voldemort, whom he was hosting in his body under his foul-smelling turban. Voldemort was kept alive by unicorn blood.

When Harry looks into the Mirror of Erised, the stone drops into his pocket, but Quirrell cannot take it from him. Quirrell's skin is burned when he touches Harry. Harry is knocked out and wakes to find himself in the Hogwarts hospital wing with Dumbledore looking over him. Dumbledore explains that Quirrell could not touch Harry because Harry has protection from his mother. Since she died saving him, her love renders him untouchable by Voldemort. Dumbledore also explains that the stone dropped into Harry's pocket only because Harry did not want to use its power.

The book ends with Harry leaving Hogwarts to spend the summer with the Dursleys, who do not know that Harry is forbidden to use magic outside of school.

Rowling drew from her own experiences when creating
the Harry Potter characters.

4

How to Apply Biographical Criticism to *Harry Potter and the Sorcerer's Stone*

What Is Biographical Criticism?

Biographical criticism explores the potential connections between authors and their writing. Looking into an author's life may enrich a reader's understanding of the text. Biographical criticism may shed light on the plot, characters, or setting of a story, as these literary elements might have been influenced by real events.

A biographical critique looks at the personal history of an author and the way it is overtly and covertly reflected in that author's writings. Overt revelations are intended by the author, and covert revelations are unintended by the author. Covert revelations are of special interest to the biographical critic but can be difficult to substantiate. This connects some cases of biographical criticism with psychoanalysis—which studies dreams, experiences, and repressed thoughts—as a critic may infer things about the author's unconscious motives based on what is found in a text. In its basic form, biographical criticism can be a useful tool for interpreting or offering new points of view about a text.

Applying Biographical Criticism to *Harry Potter and the Sorcerer's Stone*

Rowling does not usually recognize connections between her life and her word as she writes. She has said, "It often isn't until I re-read what I've written that I realize where certain bits of my stories have come from."[1] Rowling's life is reflected overtly and covertly in *Harry Potter and the Sorcerer's Stone* in the characters and plot of the novel. Hermione, Ron, and Harry all represent significant aspects of Rowling's life in intended and unintended ways, and these similarities give the story an emotional dimension

---

Thesis Statement

The thesis statement in this critique states: "Rowling's life is reflected overtly and covertly in *Harry Potter and the Sorcerer's Stone* in the characters and plot of the novel. Hermione, Ron, and Harry all represent significant aspects of Rowling's life in intended and unintended ways, and these similarities give the story an emotional dimension that would not be apparent otherwise." This thesis answers the question of how Rowling's life is reflected in her work.

that would not be apparent otherwise.

Rowling admits that she was like Hermione as a young girl, which demonstrates an intentional link between Rowling's life and the novel. Rowling said, "By eleven or twelve, I might just have been a tiny bit Hermione-ish. I always felt I had to achieve, my hand always had to be the first to go up, I always had to be right. Maybe it was because I felt quite plain in comparison to my sister."[2] Rowling's concerns about measuring up shed light on Hermione's personality. As a non-pureblood Hogwarts student with Muggle parents, Hermione is unaccustomed to the magical world that is common to other students with wizards and witches for parents. She compensates by spending tremendous amounts of energy on her studies. She quickly develops a reputation for always knowing the answer. She nags Harry and Ron when they blow off homework assignments, but she often offers help too. Despite her bossiness and characterization as a "know-it-all," Hermione's hard work and loyalty

> **Argument One**
>
> The first argument of the essay states: "Rowling admits that she was like Hermione as a young girl, which demonstrates an intentional link between Rowling's life and the novel." This argument demonstrates an overt reflection, and the next argument will demonstrate a covert reflection.

Argument Two

The second point of the essay states: "Some connections between Rowling's life and her book may have started intentionally, but they carry unintentional links as well." This point highlights Rowling's intended biographical connections between Ron and her high school friend, but the author of the essay also argues Ron reflects the life of Rowling unintentionally.

make her a likable character. Rowling gives dimension to Hermione's character by weaving positive and potentially negative characteristics into Hermione's personality.

Some connections between Rowling's life and her book may have started intentionally, but they carry unintentional links as well. For example, Rowling says a high school friend named Seán influenced her characterization of Ron. However, covert links can be seen between Rowling and Ron because Ron grows up in a loving and stable family, as did Rowling. He is also poor, something Rowling experienced firsthand as a single mother. Ron's homemade sandwiches and hand-me-down clothes carry an emotional weight Rowling experienced firsthand. Furthermore, Rowling's and Seán's connections to the Harry Potter characters can illuminate plot elements in the novels. Even though they are great friends, there is an undercurrent of particular affection between Ron and Hermione that runs throughout the books. If Hermione is like

Rowling and Ron is like Seán, perhaps Rowling's fondness for her friend influenced her decision to match up the two characters that are based on herself and Seán.

<u>The similarities between Rowling and her characters give the novel emotional accuracy, especially in portions of the novel that deal with death.</u> Rowling and Harry both experience the loss of a mother. Rowling's mother died during the process of writing the first Harry Potter book. Rowling says the section in the novel about the Mirror of Erised reflects this loss. The mirror reveals the viewer's deepest desire. (*Erised* is *desire* spelled backward.) In the mirror, Harry sees himself surrounded by his parents and relatives—all people who have died. Rowling explains, "I was conscious that when I looked in the Mirror [of Erised], I would see exactly what Harry saw."[3] Rowling never told her mother about writing Harry Potter, and the Mirror of Erised reflects her regret. Similarly, gazing into the mirror gives Harry

> **Argument Three**
>
> The third point of the essay states: "The similarities between Rowling and her characters give the novel emotional accuracy, especially in portions of the novel that deal with death." The author explains that Rowling intended for the Mirror of Erised to symbolize her own longing for her mother just as it shows Harry's longing for his family.

In *Harry Potter and the Sorcerer's Stone*, Dumbledore warns Harry not to obsess about what might have been.

a glimpse of what his life might have been like had his parents survived. Rowling's sense of wonder at what could have been is infused into Harry as a theme that runs throughout the entire series.

Because Rowling has woven some of her own anxieties, struggles, and desires in her characters, these characters seem three-dimensional. The world of Harry Potter may not be real in the conventional sense, but the things the characters experience feel true. Rowling's work fuels the imagination of the reader so that readers also might face their lives with creativity.

Conclusion

This final paragraph is the conclusion of the critique. It sums up the author's arguments and partially restates the original thesis. The conclusion also provides the reader with a new thought—that Rowling's imaginative work helps readers apply their imaginations to their own lives.

Thinking Critically about *Harry Potter and the Sorcerer's Stone*

Now it is your turn to assess the critique.
Consider these questions:

1. The thesis argues that Rowling's life is represented in her characters and the plot of the story. Do you agree? Why or why not?

2. What was the most interesting argument made? What was the strongest one? What was the weakest? Were the points backed up with strong evidence from the book and the life of the author? Did the arguments support the thesis?

3. The goal of a conclusion is sometimes more than summarizing. A conclusion can also leave the reader with a new, related idea. Do you think this conclusion effectively introduces a new idea? If so, what is it?

Other Approaches

This essay is one possible way to apply biographical criticism to *Harry Potter and the Sorcerer's Stone*. What are some other ways to approach it? A person analyzing a work using biographical information looks at the intersection between the author's life and the work. Following are two alternate approaches. The first approach examines how to apply biographical criticism by comparing Rowling's experiences at school to her characters' experiences at Hogwarts. The second approach examines how one might explore Rowling's perspective on fame and the way it is portrayed in the novel.

Teaching a Future Author

In interviews, Rowling describes different teachers in her life—some who she admires, and others who she does not admire. A writer could explore the similarities and differences between some of Rowling's teachers in her life and in her books. A teacher Rowling admires was an English teacher named Miss Shepherd, who had high expectations for Rowling and taught her a great deal about writing. Rowling says Snape's character was influenced by many people, one of whom was a teacher who bullied students at Rowling's school in Tutshill.

The thesis statement for a related essay might be: Rowling's teachers provided creative material for her to use as she wrote *Harry Potter and the Sorcerer's Stone*, which highlights the importance of good educators through positive and negative examples.

The Cost of Fame

In the book, Harry must deal with the negative effects of fame. While Rowling was not famous while she wrote *Harry Potter and the Sorcerer's Stone*, some of her concerns are voiced through the characters. Mrs. Weasley forbids her children from asking Harry about his scar and his past. Snape sarcastically refers to Harry as a celebrity at Hogwarts and criticizes him for it.

The thesis statement for such an essay might be: Rowling's concerns about becoming famous are reflected in the views of different characters in *Harry Potter and the Sorcerer's Stone*.

Students place their names into the Goblet of Fire for a chance to compete in the Triwizard Tournament.

5

An Overview of
Harry Potter and the
Goblet of Fire

Harry Potter and the Goblet of Fire begins with Voldemort and his follower Wormtail planning Harry's death. Harry witnesses this in a dream and wakes up with searing pain in his scar.

Not long after, the Weasleys, Harry, and Hermione attend the Quidditch World Cup with excellent seats in the top box. They meet Winky, the house-elf of Mr. Crouch, an important official at the Ministry of Magic. Winky is saving Mr. Crouch a seat even though she is afraid of heights. Ireland plays Bulgaria and wins.

Later, mayhem is caused when Voldemort's followers, Death Eaters, torture non-magical people. In the chaos, Harry loses his wand. Winky is found holding it near the scene where someone conjured Voldemort's sign in the sky. Mr. Crouch blames and dismisses her even though others doubt she could have done it.

Changes at Hogwarts

At Hogwarts, students are surprised to learn that the school will host the Triwizard Tournament. Students from three schools will compete against one another. Another change is that the eccentric Mad-Eye Moody is the new Defense Against the Dark Arts teacher. He aggressively teaches the unforgivable curses to students. And in response to the mistreatment of Winky, Hermione forms the Society for the Promotion of Elvish Welfare (S.P.E.W.) but has trouble recruiting members. Even Harry and Ron are reluctant to join.

Representatives from Beauxbatons and Durmstrang, the other schools competing in the Triwizard Tournament, arrive at Hogwarts in the fall. Competitors—who must be 17 or older— put their names into the Goblet of Fire, which is enchanted to pick one champion from each school. The three champions will compete against each other. Viktor Krum (Durmstrang), Fleur Delacour (Beauxbatons), and Cedric Diggory (Hogwarts) are chosen, but everyone is shocked when the

Goblet spits out another name: Harry Potter, who is not yet 17. The enchantments on the goblet prevent Harry from declining to compete, but he insists he did not enter. Ron does not believe him, and they stop speaking to each other. Only fellow Gryffindors are happy about Harry as a champion. Harry is very nervous about competing.

The Triwizard Tournament

Hagrid shows Harry that the first task involves dragons. Harry is certain that Viktor and Fleur know too, so he tells Cedric as well. During a late-night talk with his godfather, Sirius Black, the two express concern about someone putting Harry's name in the Goblet of Fire. However, Harry does well on the first task. He summons his broom and captures the dragon's golden egg, which has a clue for the second task. Ron finally realizes that Harry would never sign up to compete in the dangerous competition, and they make up.

Harry is happy to find Dobby, a free house-elf, working at Hogwarts. Winky is also at Hogwarts, but she is worried sick about her former master and is drinking too much. Dobby makes Harry a pair of Quidditch socks for Christmas, and Harry and

Ron give Dobby socks and a sweater Mrs. Weasley knitted.

During this time, Harry avoids trying to figure out the clue from his golden egg. The Yule Ball requires Harry to find a date, and this consumes his thoughts. When Cho Chang turns him down because she is going with Cedric, Harry takes Parvati Patil, and Ron takes her twin sister, Padma. The boys spend the evening sulking because Harry is jealous of Cedric and Cho, and Ron is jealous of Hermione and her date, Viktor. Cedric soon tells Harry to take

Ron and Harry have a miserable time at the Yule Ball with Padma and Parvati Patil.

a bath with his egg to figure out the clue, and Harry learns that for the second task, he must be able to breathe underwater for an hour.

Despite frantic research, Harry cannot discover how to complete the second underwater task. Dobby rescues Harry by giving him gillyweed that transforms him into a sea-like creature. Harry comes in last because he waits to make sure all the champions have retrieved their loved ones who are trapped underwater. When Fleur does not arrive to save her sister, Harry rescues her himself and is awarded extra points for showing moral fortitude. Only Karkaroff, the headmaster of Durmstrang, does not agree with the other judges. Later, Harry sees him fearfully showing Snape something on his arm.

Harry, Ron, and Hermione meet Sirius at Hogsmeade, while Sirius is disguised as a dog. He tells them Mr. Crouch's son died in Azkaban prison after Crouch charged him as a Death Eater. They buy Dobby socks to thank him for helping Harry. Winky, still drinking, says Mr. Crouch needs her help to guard his secret.

Shortly before the last tournament task, Mr. Crouch emerges from the Forbidden Forest behaving erratically and begs Harry and Viktor to get Dumbledore. By the time Harry does, Crouch has disappeared. Harry dreams about Voldemort in class and wakes up with severe pain in his scar. While waiting for Dumbledore in his office, Harry witnesses a court scene in Dumbledore's Pensieve, a memory keeper. Ludo Bagman, Karkaroff, and Mr. Crouch's son are on trial under suspicion of being Death Eaters. Based on the pain Harry feels in his scar, Dumbledore believes Voldemort is becoming more powerful.

Voldemort's Return

The final task of the tournament takes place in an enchanted maze filled with challenges for the champions to overcome, but Harry finds his path relatively clear. Cedric and Harry find the trophy at the same time. They decide they should share the victory, so they grab it together. However, the trophy is an enchanted portkey that magically transports them to a graveyard. Confused and unprepared, they encounter Wormtail, who immediately kills Cedric before performing a spell that makes Voldemort corporeal. Voldemort tries to kill Harry, but instead, Harry's wand makes

Voldemort's wand regurgitate the spells it last committed. Phantoms of the people Voldemort killed help Harry escape back to Hogwarts with Cedric's body.

In the confusion that follows Harry's return with Cedric's dead body, Mad-Eye Moody separates Harry from the crowd. He is actually the young Barty Crouch who did not die in Azkaban. He took Mad-Eye's form using Polyjuice Potion to serve Voldemort. He entered Harry in the tournament and helped him win so that Voldemort could use Harry's blood in the ritual that returned him to a bodily form.

Cornelius Fudge gives the order for Barty Crouch to receive a Dementor's kiss, which essentially kills him. Then Fudge and the Ministry of Magic deny Voldemort's return to power. Dumbledore tells the Hogwarts students about Voldemort despite Fudge's orders, and everyone leaves the school mourning the death of Cedric.

Not wanting his Triwizard winnings, Harry gives the prize money to Ron's twin brothers, Fred and George, so they can open a joke shop. He says people will need humor in the days ahead.

Hermione fights for the rights of house-elves in *Harry Potter and the Goblet of Fire*.

How to Apply Marxist Criticism to *Harry Potter and the Goblet of Fire*

No. 2

What Is Marxist Criticism?

Marxism was first developed by Karl Marx in response to industrialism in the nineteenth century. Marx criticized capitalism and advocated for mistreated factory workers to rise up and fight for freedom from oppression from large industries. Marxist theories provided the groundwork for communism, a political system in which ownership of goods, services, and their production and distribution is shared.

Marxist literary critics explore the way texts either contribute to existing class struggles in a culture or work against it. A Marxist critic might emphasize class struggles within a work or the class struggles in the time period in which a work was written. Additionally, Marxist criticism often overlaps with other types of criticism that deal with oppressed groups, such as postcolonial criticism, feminist criticism, and race theory.

Applying Marxist Criticism to *Harry Potter and the Goblet of Fire*

The Harry Potter series may exist in a magical world, but it reflects the class struggles experienced in the readers' world. Wizards have money and money trouble. There are also oppressed classes within the wizarding community, including giants, centaurs, goblins, and house-elves. House-elves are slaves typically bound to old, rich wizarding families and are usually treated poorly. Because house-elves were not always enslaved and because they show themselves as able to act with intelligence and independence, it is appropriate to consider how their struggles may relate to the world inhabited by readers. The challenge of alleviating oppression and class struggle is illustrated in the lives of two

Thesis Statement

The thesis statement in this critique states: "The challenge of alleviating oppression and class struggle is illustrated in the lives of two house-elves in *Harry Potter and the Goblet of Fire*, Winky and Dobby, as well as in Hermione's struggle to help them. Despite these difficulties, the book shows that social and economic progress can be made when relationships are built across class lines." This thesis answers the question: Does *Harry Potter and the Goblet of Fire* reinforce or challenge the existing class system?

house-elves in *Harry Potter and the Goblet of Fire*, Winky and Dobby, as well as in Hermione's struggle to help them. Despite these difficulties, the book shows that social and economic progress can be made when relationships are built across class lines.

Hermione's concern for the well-being of house-elves is incited by her exposure to Winky and the plight of house-elves in general, but she has trouble finding others who share her concern. When Barty Crouch dismisses Winky, believing she conjured Voldemort's Dark Mark, Hermione is outraged by the way Winky is treated. Hermione is even more upset to discover Hogwarts uses house-elves for labor. Even though house-elves are treated well at Hogwarts, illustrated when both Dobby and Winky find work there and Dobby is paid, Hermione wants more protections for them. She creates S.P.E.W. with the goal of getting elves fair wages and working conditions and to work toward their representation in the Ministry of Magic. Ultimately, she wants to repeal the law

> **Argument One**
>
> The first point of this essay states: "Hermione's concern for the well-being of house-elves is incited by her exposure to Winky and the plight of house-elves in general, but she has trouble finding others who share her concern." The author supports this argument with examples of Hermione's difficulties.

Argument Two

The second point of the essay states: "Another complication to Hermione's plan is that she cannot find interest in S.P.E.W. among the elves." The author points out that history has shown that oppressed groups may not seek change due to fear or because their oppression becomes familiar. She is continuing to draw parallels between the real world and the magical world in Rowling's books.

against elves using wands, but no one wants to join S.P.E.W.—even Harry and Ron are reluctant.

Another complication to Hermione's plan is that she cannot find interest in S.P.E.W. among the elves. Winky is ashamed by her freedom and is devastated by leaving the Crouch family. Dobby is ostracized by his fellow house-elves because of his liberal ideas, which lead him to being paid and receiving time off. The house-elves' attitudes represent what Marx called an ideology, or a belief system. Marx argued that oppressed classes are often unable to overcome their oppression because they begin to identify with that oppression. Marx claimed that this identification was the result of an ideology. Professor and author Jack Zipes asks, "Is Rowling trying to show that workers have such a low political consciousness that they will not listen to an enlightened leader like Hermione?"[1] The house-elves' reluctance to change is reflected in the actual world. Some who are enslaved and

colonized promote the process because they become
accustomed to the mistreatment they receive.
They have been transformed by the ideology that
they belong in the lower class. Even after he is
freed, Dobby struggles to stop
physically punishing himself if
he speaks badly about his former
masters.

Draco Malfoy,
left, speaks with
Viktor Krum.
Draco is part
of a wealthy
wizarding family
that owns house-
elves.

The lives of the house-elves
and the wizards improve when
they develop relationships with
one another across class lines.
Dobby's relationship with Harry

Argument Three
The third point of the essay
states: "The lives of the
house-elves and the wizards
improve when they develop
relationships with one another
across class lines." The
author argues that Dobby's
relationship with Harry
illustrates this point.

strengthens after Harry frees him in book two of the series. In *Harry Potter and the Goblet of Fire*, Dobby finds employment at Hogwarts, and he and Harry exchange Christmas gifts. Harry is able to succeed in the tournament's second task when Dobby gives him the gillyweed that helps him breathe underwater. After Dobby helps Harry in the tournament, Harry, Ron, and Hermione also thank him with gifts.

> **Conclusion**
>
> This final paragraph is the conclusion of the critique. It sums up the author's arguments and partially restates the original thesis, which has now been argued and supported with evidence from the text. The conclusion reiterates the idea that Rowling might have been offering potential solutions for how to solve problems between classes.

While the enslavement of house-elves and the status of other marginalized groups does not change in a systematic way in the Harry Potter books, the lines dividing the classes become blurred when care and community are developed among the characters. The book reveals underlying themes relating to class struggle and potential solutions for oppression.

Thinking Critically about *Harry Potter and the Goblet of Fire*

Now it is your turn to assess the critique.

Consider these questions:

1. The thesis argues that while it is a challenge to make changes in class inequities, relationships help break down the barriers between classes. Do you agree? Why or why not?

2. What was the most interesting argument made? What was the strongest one? What was the weakest? Were the points backed up with strong evidence from the book? Did the arguments support the thesis?

3. Do you agree with the conclusion? Can you think of any other evidence from the book that could be used to support a Marxist reading of the text? Are there other instances of class struggle in the Harry Potter series?

Other Approaches

The essay you just read is one possible way to apply Marxist criticism to a critique of *Harry Potter and the Goblet of Fire*. What are some other ways you could approach it? Analyzing a work using Marxist criticism looks at the intersection between Marxist ideas and the work. Following are two alternate approaches. The first approach examines the connection between Voldemort's quest to purify the wizarding race and the real world of readers. The second explores Rowling's class struggles.

Anti-Winning

Voldemort's quest to purify the wizarding community of Muggles and Muggle-born witches and wizards is carried on by his followers. This reflects the power the rich and educated have over others in real-life society. But the sense of superiority one might sense wizards and witches have over humans in the books is counterpointed by the way Harry undermines competition in the Triwizard Tournament.

The thesis statement for a related essay might be: While wizards and witches can dominate others the way educated and rich people can in the actual world, Harry resists this tendency by undermining competition in the Triwizard Tournament when he protects others and emphasizes justice.

Striving for Success

Rowling's personal history affects her understanding of class. Her father was a factory worker and then became a manager, shifting from a working-class job to a professional position. As an adult, Rowling also shifted from her role as a teacher, wife, and mother to a divorced and unemployed mother. Then she shifted again to become a famous, wealthy author. Fred and George Weasley's struggles to start their own business reflect Rowling's money struggles. Rather than striving for social change, Fred and George Weasley and Rowling strive to change their economic circumstances, thereby reinforcing the class system.

The thesis statement for a related essay might be: In her own life and in the lives of the characters, Rowling reinforces the class system by focusing on how to achieve economic success rather than redistribute wealth and overthrow the class system.

Fans attend the premiere of *Harry Potter and the Half-Blood Prince* in London in July 2009.

Chapter 7

An Overview of
Harry Potter and the Half-Blood Prince

At the start of the book, Snape makes an unbreakable vow with Death Eater Narcissa Malfoy to aid her son, Draco, in the mysterious task Voldemort has given him. At the same time, Harry struggles to embrace the prophecy that says he must kill or be killed by Voldemort. Harry also mourns the death of his godfather, Sirius.

In Diagon Alley, Harry, Hermione, and Ron follow Draco to a Dark Arts shop named Borgin and Burkes, where they overhear Draco threatening an employee. Harry believes Draco has become a Death Eater.

Studying Voldemort

Back at Hogwarts, Harry studies Potions with a new teacher, Professor Slughorn. Slughorn believes

Harry is gifted in the subject. However, Harry's skill is dependent upon the notes he finds in an old textbook that was once owned by the unknown Half-Blood Prince.

In private lessons, Dumbledore shares information about Voldemort's personal history. Harry and Dumbledore journey into memories in Dumbledore's Pensieve. Voldemort's mother, Merope, was part of an inbred, violent wizarding family obsessed with its purebred bloodlines, but she married a handsome Muggle. He left her while she was pregnant.

Meanwhile, Harry clings to the belief that Draco smuggled something into school. A visit to the town of Hogsmeade is marred by the mystery surrounding a cursed necklace that puts a student's life in danger. Harry tries to implicate Draco in the incident without success.

Delving further into Voldemort's history, Dumbledore and Harry discover Voldemort's desperate, pregnant mother sold a locket passed down from the famous Salazar Slytherin for a small sum of wizard gold, not knowing how much the locket was worth. She died at an orphanage birthing her son, naming him Tom Marvolo Riddle.

Dumbledore also shares his memory of first meeting the young Tom at this orphanage. Tom could already use his magic to control people.

After a terrible Quidditch practice, Harry and Ron encounter Ginny Weasley and her boyfriend, Dean Thomas, kissing in a hallway. Harry's pent-up interest in Ginny is unleashed when he sees Ginny kiss Dean. Hermione warns Harry that girls are sneaking in banned love potions to use on Harry. Harry believes this suggests Draco is smuggling Dark objects into school. Poisoned mead intended for Dumbledore is accidentally given to Ron, supporting Harry's theory.

Horcruxes

At Slughorn's Christmas party, Harry eavesdrops on Draco and Snape arguing about the task Voldemort assigned to Draco. Snape offers to help Draco, but Draco accuses Snape of wanting the glory. Over Christmas break at the Weasley home, everyone thinks Snape is pretending to help Draco in order to help Dumbledore's Order of the Phoenix. Harry discovers that if Snape does not honor his unbreakable vow, he will die.

After Christmas, Harry cannot interest Dumbledore in his theory about Draco. Dumbledore

says it is not important. Dumbledore then reveals
Voldemort was obsessed with his parentage and
probably framed his uncle Morfin for murder before
stealing a treasured family ring. In the Pensieve,
Harry sees young Tom ask Slughorn about
Horcruxes in a memory Slughorn tampered with.
Dumbledore asks Harry to retrieve the true memory
from Slughorn, stressing it is the most important
memory yet. When Harry asks Slughorn directly,
Slughorn angrily says there was nothing more to the
memory.

Harry becomes fixated on Draco again. He
pores over his enchanted Marauder's Map that
shows the location of everyone in Hogwarts and
discovers Draco is disappearing off the map. Losing
interest in Quidditch, Harry uses house-elves
Kreacher and Dobby to follow Draco.

Disappointed that Harry has not acquired
Slughorn's true memory, Dumbledore explains they
are limited without it. They learn Tom worked for
Borgin and Burkes after graduating from Hogwarts
and stole Helga Hufflepuff's cup and Salazar
Slytherin's locket from a client. They also view
the memory of Tom unsuccessfully asking to teach
Defense Against the Dark Arts at Hogwarts.

Kreacher and Dobby report Draco is using the Room of Requirement. Harry finds he cannot access it as it is when Draco uses it. Hermione reminds Harry that his best chance of doing something useful is getting the memory from Slughorn. Ron tells him to use the luck potion Harry won from Slughorn. Harry does not admit his secret desire to use it to split up Ginny and Dean.

Harry and Dumbledore explore Voldemort's history in Dumbledore's Pensieve.

The True Memory

Under the effects of the potion, Ginny actually does break up with Dean, and Harry convinces a drunken Slughorn to give him the memory. The memory shows Tom asking a horrified Slughorn about Horcruxes. Slughorn tells Tom that wizards use Horcruxes to hide a splinter of their soul after committing murder. To Slughorn's astonishment, Tom suggests it would be good to split the soul seven times.

Dumbledore and Harry are convinced Voldemort created seven Horcruxes, the first being the diary that possessed Ginny in the second book of the series, and the second being the family ring he stole. Dumbledore destroyed the ring, and in doing so, destroyed his own hand. Dumbledore and Harry speculate the other Horcruxes are the Slytherin locket, the Hufflepuff cup, something from Godric Gryffindor or Rowena Ravenclaw, and Voldemort's snake, Nagini. The seventh Horcrux is revealed in the final book.

When Harry finds Draco crying in the bathroom and they duel, Harry is horrified by the effect of a spell the Half-Blood Prince designed, which slashes Draco with deep cuts. Snape finds them in time to save Draco's life. Harry gets detention, causing him to miss Quidditch. Ginny takes his place as seeker. The team wins, and Harry and Ginny kiss.

Death of the Headmaster

Harry learns that years ago, Snape told Voldemort about the prophecy, which resulted in the murder of Harry's parents. Dumbledore insists on trusting Snape and offers to let Harry go with him to find a Horcrux. Harry is concerned about leaving because he believes Draco is close to completing his task. Harry gives his friends the rest of his luck potion and tells them to look out.

Harry and Dumbledore find the cave where Voldemort hid the Horcrux—a locket. It is protected by enchantments. Dumbledore is severely weakened by poisoned water, but the two obtain the Horcrux. When they return to Hogwarts, Draco is waiting on a tall tower. He has used a magic closet to transport Death Eaters to Hogwarts through the Room of Requirement, and he intends to kill Dumbledore. He cannot bring himself to do it, and Snape kills Dumbledore instead. In the battle that follows, Harry finds out that Snape is the Half-Blood Prince.

As a result of Dumbledore's death, Harry decides to drop out of school to look for the remaining Horcruxes. He breaks up with Ginny because he says Voldemort might use her to get to him, but Ron and Hermione insist on joining him.

Throughout *Harry Potter and the Half-Blood Prince*, Harry represses his desire for Ginny.

How to Apply Psychoanalytic Criticism to *Harry Potter and the Half-Blood Prince*

No.2

What Is Psychoanalytic Criticism?

A psychoanalytic critic explores literature using the principles of psychoanalysis first developed by Austrian psychologist Sigmund Freud (1856–1939). Freud emphasized the influence of the unconscious part of the human mind on human behavior. The unconscious mind harbors drives such as aggression and sexuality. While infants reflect their drives and passions without restraint, Freud believed children are socialized so that certain drives and urges are repressed when necessary. This helps them learn to fit into adult society. A Freudian critic often looks for the effects of repressed desires in the characters of a text or its author.

Applying Psychoanalytic Criticism to *Harry Potter and the Half-Blood Prince*

It is certainly understandable that a character such as Harry Potter would repress memories, emotions, and desires. Not only is he an orphan whose parents were murdered, but he also witnesses the deaths of Cedric, Sirius, and eventually, his headmaster Dumbledore. But fundamentally, the death he has to grapple with the most is his own. He has learned that according to a prophecy, he will engage in a fight to the death with Voldemort. This renders him unable to focus on "normal" teenage things. Throughout *Harry Potter and the Half-Blood Prince*, Harry represses his love for Ginny and his fears about his upcoming fight with Voldemort. The outlet for these repressed feelings is his obsession with the secret plans of Draco and Snape.

Harry's repressed feelings for Ginny assert themselves

Thesis Statement

This thesis statement argues: "Throughout *Harry Potter and the Half-Blood Prince*, Harry represses his love for Ginny and his fears about his upcoming fight with Voldemort. The outlet for these repressed feelings is his obsession with the secret plans of Draco and Snape." This thesis addresses the questions: What are Harry's repressed fears and desires, and how are they manifested in his behavior? This thesis argues that he focuses on Draco and Snape because he does not want to face his fear of Voldemort and his love for Ginny.

when he discovers a love potion that smells like her. In Slughorn's Potions class, Hermione explains that a love potion is "supposed to smell differently to each of us, according to what attracts us."[1] When Harry smells the love potion, he finds it smells like treacle tart, a broomstick handle, "and something flowery he thought he might have smelled at the Burrow [Ginny's home]."[2] He catches the flowery scent again when Ginny arrives at dinner.

The more Harry represses his interest in Ginny and his assignment to obtain Slughorn's original memory about Voldemort and Horcruxes, the more consumed he becomes with Draco's plans. Even though Dumbledore tells Harry that Slughorn's memory is essential, Harry does not put all his energy into the task because he is not

Argument One

The author of this essay has begun to argue her thesis by stating: "Harry's repressed feelings for Ginny assert themselves when he discovers a love potion that smells like her." The author is providing evidence that Harry really loves Ginny, but his feelings dwell in his unconscious mind.

Argument Two

The second argument of the essay states: "The more Harry represses his interest in Ginny and his assignment to obtain Slughorn's original memory about Voldemort and Horcruxes, the more consumed he becomes with Draco's plans." The author lists the ways Harry obsesses about Draco and how this outlet helps him ignore his feelings for Ginny and his anxiety about facing Voldemort.

ready to face his fear of mortality. After asking for the memory once, Slughorn becomes defensive and avoids Harry. So Harry ignores the task. It is a direct reminder of his upcoming fight with Voldemort, and he represses his fear by avoiding it. Pouring over his Marauder's Map, he obsesses about where Draco goes. He even begins to act a bit neurotic when he assigns Kreacher and Dobby to follow Draco and when he loses interest in Quidditch.

Harry's obsession with Draco creates an outlet for his repressed fears and pent-up frustration about facing Voldemort as well as his repressed desire for Ginny. Focusing on Draco becomes what Freud called a compromise formation and an inversion. Freud explains that neurotic behaviors "frequently displace desires, or anxieties, or drive energies that are unconscious onto expressive activities or compulsive thoughts."[3] When Harry neurotically focuses on Draco, he indirectly expresses his drive

Argument Three

The third argument of the essay states: "Harry's obsession with Draco creates an outlet for his repressed fears and pent-up frustration about facing Voldemort as well as his repressed desire for Ginny." The author develops the concept of repression by further arguing that his feelings about fighting Voldemort are displaced through his focus on Draco. She also explains that when Harry acts on his desire for Ginny, he inverts his hate for Voldemort by concentrating on the opposite: love.

Harry spends much of the book tracking and thinking about Draco Malfoy.

to fight Voldemort and his repressed fears about that fight. Therefore, obsessing about Draco is a compromise formation releasing pent-up energy about Harry's pending battle to the death with Voldemort. Additionally, Harry's interest in Draco is an inversion of his interest in Ginny. Rather than focusing on someone he loves, he focuses on someone he hates. However, the inversion shifts when he engages briefly in a relationship with Ginny. Then, he inverts his hatred for Voldemort into his interest for Ginny.

When Draco and Snape's assassination plans for Dumbledore are exposed and executed, Harry's

Argument Four

The fourth argument of the essay states: "When Draco and Snape's assassination plans for Dumbledore are exposed and executed, Harry's compromise formation crumbles and with it, his attempts at inversion." The author argues that Harry finally embraces death.

compromise formation crumbles and with it, his attempts at inversion. The compromise formation and the inversion are not strong enough to repress Harry's need to face his own death or kill Voldemort. In the wake of Dumbledore's death, Harry decides to concentrate solely on destroying Voldemort's Horcruxes, knowing it will bring him closer to defeating Voldemort. Harry tells Ginny he cannot be involved with her because Voldemort might use her against him. He must steel himself for death by shutting out love.

Conclusion

This is the conclusion of the critique. The conclusion provides the reader with a new thought—that repression techniques cannot last.

Obsessing about Draco and Snape helps Harry express some of his pent-up fear about his fight with Voldemort. Repressing his desire for Ginny helps him face his own mortality. However, at the end of the book, Harry's repression methods have collapsed. This shows that although repression can work for a short time, true desires will ultimately break through to the surface.

Thinking Critically about *Harry Potter and the Half-Blood Prince*

Now it is your turn to assess the critique.
Consider these questions:

1. The thesis argues that Harry fixates on the plans of Draco and Snape because he is repressing his love for Ginny and his fear of mortality. Do you agree? Why or why not?

2. Can you think of any additional clues from the text that could support the thesis? Can you think of any evidence that could disprove the thesis? What are they?

3. The conclusion should restate the thesis and summarize the arguments of the essay. Does this conclusion do that effectively? Why or why not? Do you agree with the author's statement that repression tactics will ultimately fail?

Other Approaches

The essay you read is one possible way to apply psychoanalytic criticism to *Harry Potter and the Half-Blood Prince*. What are some other ways to approach it? Analyzing a work using psychoanalytic criticism looks at the intersection between the ideas of psychoanalysis and the work. Following are two alternate approaches. The first approach examines Harry's repressed feelings toward Voldemort. The second approach examines Voldemort's repressed fear of the unknown: death.

Compassion for the Dark Lord

Harry feels an inkling of sorrow for Voldemort, whose mother not only died in childbirth, but also did not use magic to save herself for the sake of her son. Dumbledore asks Harry: "Could you possibly be feeling sorry for Lord Voldemort?"[4] Harry quickly says no, but he seems to recognize the similar heartbreak of being raised without a mother. This is something he and Voldemort share.

The thesis statement for analyzing the way Harry unconsciously identifies and sympathizes with Lord Voldemort might be the following: Harry does not want to face the similarities between his story and Voldemort's, and he represses his

compassion for the infant whose mother died unable
to protect her baby.

Defying Death, Denying Life

Voldemort refuses to face his own death and
believes magic should protect people from death. In
Dumbledore's first meeting with Tom long before
he becomes Lord Voldemort, Tom says, "My mother
can't have been magic, or she wouldn't have died."[5]
Tom creates Horcruxes to avoid death, even at the
cost of ripping his soul. Most of his life is spent
creating and hiding Horcruxes — a process that
involves murder. His repressed fears of death seem
to keep him from enjoying life.

The thesis statement for an essay analyzing
Voldemort's repressed fear of death might be:
Voldemort represses his fear of death by fixating on
making Horcruxes, which inevitably, and ironically,
reduces his ability to enjoy the life he has.

Partway through the final Harry Potter book, an argument causes Ron to leave Harry and Hermione as they track Voldemort's Horcruxes.

An Overview of
Harry Potter and the
Deathly Hallows

The last book of the series begins with Harry
preparing to leave the Dursleys' home for good.
For security, his friends take Polyjuice Potion to
become decoy duplicates of Harry as they leave.
Each "Harry" travels with one member of the Order
of the Phoenix. Because Snape has tipped them off,
Death Eaters attack them immediately. In the attack,
Harry's wand acts of its own accord to save him
from Voldemort.

Mad-Eye Moody does not survive the attack,
and George Weasley permanently loses an ear.
The connection between Harry's and Voldemort's
minds reestablishes itself, and Harry experiences
Voldemort's inquisition of a wand maker to figure
out why he could not kill Harry even when using a
borrowed wand.

The Hunt for Horcruxes

In the midst of planning Bill Weasley's wedding to Fleur Delacour, Ron, Hermione, and Harry make plans to find and destroy Voldemort's remaining Horcruxes. Dumbledore leaves them mysterious gifts in his will: a Deluminator, a book of fairy tales, a snitch, and the sword of Gryffindor. The Ministry of Magic will not give Harry the sword because it did not actually belong to Dumbledore.

At Fleur and Bill's wedding, Death Eaters attack because Voldemort has taken over the Ministry of Magic. Hermione, Ron, and Harry Disapparate quickly. Thanks to Hermione, they have important supplies in an enchanted handbag. They find safe haven in the former home of Sirius, which has been left to Harry. The heavy enchantments surrounding the house shield them from discovery. Here, they befriend the Blacks' house-elf, Kreacher, and solve the mystery of the fake Horcrux that Harry and Dumbledore had retrieved before Dumbledore's death. Sirius's brother, Regulus, was a Death Eater. Regulus allowed Voldemort to use Kreacher to hide a locket of Salazar Slytherin's that Voldemort had turned into a Horcrux. Later, when Regulus recanted being a Death Eater, he stole the Horcrux locket with Kreacher's help and replaced it with a fake locket. However, Mundungus Fletcher stole the Horcrux locket from Kreacher, and a Ministry official took it from him. Harry, Ron, and Hermione break into the Ministry of Magic and get the locket.

After escaping from the Ministry, a Death Eater penetrates Sirius's house, so the friends cannot return there safely. Instead, they camp in the woods in a magical tent. Over time, they become frustrated by the lack of food and information about where the next Horcrux is hidden. Furthermore, they do not know how to destroy the Horcrux they have. They take turns wearing the locket and find that the sliver of Voldemort's soul has a strong negative effect on them. Harry continues to enter Voldemort's mind and learns he is looking for someone who stole an important wand.

Overhearing the conversation of a goblin, Hermione, Ron, and Harry discover the sword of Gryffindor can destroy Horcruxes and that the sword is no longer at Hogwarts. A fake sword has been planted at Hogwarts, and Harry wants to find the original one. Ron and Harry fight when Ron expresses his disappointment about the journey. He leaves Hermione and Harry, who are devastated.

Defeat and Triumph

Harry finally convinces Hermione to visit his hometown where his parents were murdered. After visiting their graves, Harry is tricked by an old friend of Dumbledore's family, Bathilda Bagshot. Believing she can give them Gryffindor's sword, they discover she is dead, and Voldemort's snake, Nagini, is hiding in her body to attack them. They escape, but Harry's wand is destroyed in the attack.

Bathilda Bagshot lures Harry and Hermione into her home before transforming into Voldemort's snake, Nagini.

Harry and Hermione recover and regroup, and Harry finds his magical abilities limited by the borrowed wand he is using. Furthermore, Rita

Skeeter's biography of Dumbledore confuses Harry.
Despite knowing Skeeter will lie to make a story
more dramatic, Harry still worries about her claims
that Dumbledore was close friends with the Dark
wizard Grindelwald and that Dumbledore may
have caused his own sister's death. A picture of
the young Grindelwald reveals that he is the man
Voldemort is seeking about a wand.

One night, Harry follows the Patronus of a
doe, which leads him to the sword of Gryffindor
at the bottom of an icy pond. The locket Horcrux
Harry wears strangles him as he dives in after the
sword. Ron reappears, saves Harry, and destroys the
Horcrux.

The Deathly Hallows

The friends visit Xenophilius Lovegood to ask
him about a symbol Hermione found written in the
book of fairy tales Dumbledore gave her. He tells
them the story of the Deathly Hallows, three objects
that defy death: the Elder Wand, the Resurrection
Stone, and the Invisibility Cloak.

Because Death Eaters have imprisoned
Hogwarts student Luna Lovegood, Xenophilius
turns in Harry, Hermione, and Ron hoping to get

back his daughter. After the three make a narrow escape, Harry finds himself torn between the desire to seek the Deathly Hallows and the need to find and destroy Horcruxes. Before he can make up his mind, the three are caught. Harry, Ron, and Hermione are brought to the Malfoys' home. Their wands are confiscated, leaving them vulnerable.

Due to a quick spell by Hermione, Harry's face is disfigured, and he is unrecognizable. The Malfoys are hesitant to call Voldemort, not knowing if they have actually captured Harry Potter. Horrified to see the sword of Gryffindor, believing it has been stolen from her vault at Gringotts bank, Bellatrix Lestrange tortures Hermione to find out what else may have been taken. Dobby helps Hermione escape to Bill and Fleur's home along with Harry, Ron, Luna, Griphook the goblin, and Ollivander the wand maker. Dobby is killed during the escape.

The Search Continues

After burying Dobby, Harry chooses to pursue Horcruxes over the Deathly Hallows. Enlisting the help of Griphook, Hermione, Ron, and Harry break into Gringotts. Using wands that they won in the battle at the Malfoys', they manage to acquire the Hufflepuff cup from the Lestrange vault and escape on the back of a dragon. Griphook takes the sword of Gryffindor with him, which Harry said he could have in exchange for his help but did not plan to give to him before using it to destroy the Horcrux.

Through his connection to Voldemort's mind, Harry learns that a Horcrux is hidden somewhere at Hogwarts and that Dumbledore had the Elder Wand. Harry maintains his decision to search for Horcruxes as Voldemort steals the wand.

When they arrive at Hogwarts, they meet a resistance force of students in the enchanted Room of Requirement. Neville Longbottom summons others he knows want to fight Voldemort. Ravenclaw students help Harry conclude the lost diadem of Rowena Ravenclaw must be a Horcrux. Harry, Ron, and Hermione find it and destroy it with a Basilisk fang, while a battle with Voldemort's followers rages.

Snape Vindicated

Voldemort calls a cease-fire, asking Hogwarts defenders to give up Harry. In the tense calm, Harry, Ron, and Hermione overhear Voldemort telling

Snape the Elder Wand does not seem very powerful. Voldemort orders his snake, Nagini, to kill Snape. Because Snape killed Dumbledore, the previous master of the wand, Voldemort hopes the wand will offer allegiance to him when Snape dies.

As Snape dies, Harry collects Snape's memories and rushes to view them in Dumbledore's Pensieve. Snape's memories reveal that his deep love for Harry's mother, Lily Potter, fueled all his actions after she died. Snape devoted himself to protecting Harry, acting as a double agent for Dumbledore to the very end. He never wavered in his love for Lily, but never revealed to anyone but Dumbledore that he was protecting Harry.

Harry also discovers that part of Voldemort's soul resides in Harry, making him a Horcrux. In order to destroy the Horcrux within himself, Harry gives himself over to Voldemort to be killed so that Voldemort may eventually be destroyed by another. However, Voldemort's killing curse does not actually kill Harry.

Harry winds up in a transitional state hovering between life and death. Dumbledore meets him in this place to reveal that because Voldemort used Harry's blood to become corporeal, he could not kill Harry. Part of the protective enchantment that resided in Harry from his mother resides in Voldemort, keeping Harry alive. Harry makes the choice to come back and fight instead of going on.

The Final Battle

Believing Harry is dead, Voldemort displays his body to the resistance in the hope of discouraging them. In the fight that follows, Neville kills Nagini, the final Horcrux. Harry eventually faces Voldemort. He asks Voldemort to recant and reveals Snape's true nature. He also reveals that he is using Draco's wand, which he won in the battle at the Malfoys' home. Because it was Draco's wand that disarmed Dumbledore before death, Harry rightly assumes the Elder Wand will recognize Harry as master. This allows Harry's spell to defeat Voldemort. Voldemort is defeated when his own killing curse rebounds off Harry's spell. Harry buries the Elder Wand with Dumbledore—but not before using it to repair his own broken wand.

The Epilogue takes readers forward 19 years as Harry and Ginny send off their children on the Hogwarts Express. Ron and Hermione also send off their own children.

Throughout the Harry Potter series, it is unclear if Snape is loyal to Dumbledore or to Voldemort.

How to Apply Structuralism to *Harry Potter and the Deathly Hallows*

No.2

What Is Structuralism?

Structuralist critics focus on the way meaning is created through the language used in a text. Critics applying structuralism also look for meaning in the text by considering its relationship to other structures, such as a literary genre. Regarding structuralism, author Peter Barry says, "Its essence is the belief that things cannot be understood in isolation—they have to be seen in the context of the larger structures they are part of."[1]

Structuralists may look for the way meaning is created through word pairs that are opposites. These pairs are referred to as binary oppositions or dyads, and they include concepts such as good/ evil, love/hate, and strength/weakness. While structuralists argue that meaning is created through the relationships between words, they often propose that one word in the dyad will dominate the other.

Applying Structuralism to *Harry Potter and the Deathly Hallows*

The relationship between good and evil is clearly central to the Harry Potter series. While it may be complicated to define good and evil in general terms, most characters are easily categorized as those who support Voldemort, who embodies evil, or those who support Harry, who embodies good. In the final book, *Harry Potter and the Deathly Hallows*, it is Harry who has the final triumph. Good, which is associated with love, is clearly the dominant item in this oppositional pairing of good and evil. However, within individual characters, the struggle between good and evil is also seen. The internal struggle between good and evil is balanced with such complexity in Snape's character that it is difficult to determine which aspect of this dyad is emphasized over the other. Ultimately, goodness dominates in Snape

Thesis Statement

The thesis statement in this critique states: "Ultimately, goodness dominates in Snape because his love for Lily drives his every move, showing that good is stronger than evil." This thesis statement addresses the question: Which part dominates in the oppositional pairing of good and evil in Snape's character? The arguments prove good, through love, is dominant.

because his love for Lily drives his every move, showing that good is stronger than evil.

Snape is drawn to good through his love for Lily. Through the Pensieve, the reader witnesses Snape's adolescent years. He develops a love for Lily, who represents the good side of magic. Because Lily's parents are Muggles, she knows nothing about the wizarding world. Snape is her first connection to this new world, and their bond with one another grows as he tells her about the wizarding community she will join. They stay friends throughout much of their life at Hogwarts. However, a tension grows because the two are in different houses and have different interests. Lily confronts Snape about his association with Voldemort's Death Eaters, but she still considers him her friend until he deeply insults her. Years later, after Snape tells Voldemort about a prophecy that Harry will become a mortal foe to Voldemort, it becomes Snape's deepest regret because it leads to Lily's death. Even after her death, Snape's love for

> **Argument One**
>
> The author of this essay has begun to argue the thesis. Her first argument states: "Snape is drawn to good through his love for Lily." This point begins to address the tension between good and evil by showing how Snape is drawn to good through his love of another character.

Lily is so intense that his Patronus charm takes the same form as hers: a doe.

<u>While he loves Lily, Snape is drawn to evil because of the acceptance and power he finds with the Death Eaters.</u> Snape is a social outcast who is often described as greasy-haired and awkward. A Pensieve scene earlier in the series shows Harry's young father, James Potter, tormenting Snape as other Gryffindor students laugh. Clearly, Snape does not fit in with most of his peers. However, Snape finds acceptance in the Slytherin house, which is associated with the Death Eaters and the Dark Arts. Snape becomes a successful wizard with a talent for potion making. In a previous book, it is revealed that Snape is the Half-Blood Prince who creates a dangerous and violent spell. As an adult, Snape continues to favor Dark magic by repeatedly applying to teach Defense Against the Dark Arts. Dumbledore turns him down time after time.

> **Argument Two**
>
> The second argument in the essay states: "While he loves Lily, Snape is drawn to evil because of the acceptance and power he finds with the Death Eaters." This point addresses the other side of the tension between good and evil by showing that despite loving Lily, Snape is drawn to evil through a lust for power.

Furthermore, Snape is drawn to the evil Voldemort because they have similar histories. Both are outcasts. Voldemort is an orphan who grew up in a children's home. Although his mother was magical, his father was a Muggle. This causes an identity crisis for Voldemort, who surrounds himself with pureblood wizards and seems ashamed of his half-blood status. In his youth, Snape has an unhappy home life and is continually teased by his classmates and called nicknames by James and his friends. Power, especially gained through the Dark Arts, is appealing to these two men. This lust for power, combined with their outcast backgrounds, link them in a bent toward evil.

Ultimately, however, Snape chooses his love for Lily over his alliance with Voldemort, symbolically choosing good over evil. By the end of the novel, it is clear that every action

Argument Three

The third argument of the essay states: "Furthermore, Snape is drawn to the evil Voldemort because they have similar histories." This point gives additional weight to the evil side of Snape by aligning him with the most evil character in the book.

Argument Four

The fourth argument of the essay states: "Ultimately, however, Snape chooses his love for Lily over his alliance with Voldemort, symbolically choosing good over evil." This final argument addresses what Lily and Voldemort symbolize. The author equates each character with one side of the binary pair of good and evil.

Throughout the series, Snape appears to be Harry's enemy, punishing him and his friends any chance he gets.

of Snape's was driven by his love for Lily, who symbolizes good. In a plot twist, it is revealed that when Snape murdered Dumbledore, it was actually done in loyalty to the headmaster and his Order of the Phoenix. Significantly, Snape also helps Harry acquire Gryffindor's sword that enables Harry to destroy Voldemort's Horcruxes.

Love is closely associated with good in the series, and hatred is closely associated with evil. Dumbledore argues that Harry's capacity to love is his greatest strength, and Voldemort's movement is based on the hatred of Muggles and magical people born from Muggles. Despite his hatred for Harry and James, Snape's love for Lily drives him to align with the good side of magic and significantly contribute to the destruction of the evil Voldemort. If Snape can overrule his hatred for Harry enough to see Lily in him, then love wins over hate. As Snape dies, he demands that Harry look him in the eye, knowing Harry's eyes are just like Lily's. Snape seeks the eyes of the person he hates most to remember the one he loved more than anyone. Perhaps it is here that readers see the balance tip in favor of love. A few scenes later, Voldemort is destroyed.

Fundamentally, goodness wins in the Harry Potter series. Even in Snape, the balance between good and evil tips in favor of love and goodness. But as a character, Snape highlights the fine line between

> **Conclusion**
> This final paragraph is the conclusion of the critique. The conclusion reiterates the thesis and the author's arguments. A new thought has also been introduced—that the line between love and hate might be flexible and unstable.

In *Harry Potter and the Prisoner of Azkaban*, Snape briefly protects Harry and his friends. In the final book, it is revealed that Snape had been working on Harry's behalf all along.

the oppositional pairs: the place they overlap, the place where the distinction between love and hate is flexible and unstable.

Thinking Critically about *Harry Potter and the Deathly Hallows*

Now it is your turn to assess the critique. Consider these questions:

1. The thesis argues that goodness and love are stronger in Snape than evil and hate. Do you agree? Why or why not?

2. What was the strongest argument presented? Can you think of any evidence to use against it? What is it?

3. Do you agree or disagree with the author's assertion in the conclusion that the distinction between love and hate is often unstable? Does the evidence from the text support or refute this claim?

Other Approaches

This essay is one possible way to apply structuralism to *Harry Potter and the Deathly Hallows*, but there are other ways to approach the text. Analyzing a work using structuralism looks at the way outside structures affect the work. Following are two alternate approaches. The first approach examines the oppositional pairing of two characters—Molly Weasley and Bellatrix Lestrange. The second approach explores how *Harry Potter and the Deathly Hallows* relates to the genre of fairy tales.

Masterful Mother

Pairing characters can create oppositional dyads. With Molly Weasley and Bellatrix Lestrange, we see a pairing of good and evil embodied in the lives of two characters.

A thesis statement for a structuralist critique analyzing the struggle between good and evil portrayed between Molly Weasley and Bellatrix Lestrange might be the following: While Molly Weasley is often portrayed in a comic fashion as a harried mother, she demonstrates her powerful skills as a witch and dominates the fight of good over evil in her duel against Bellatrix Lestrange.

The Fairy Tale and Harry

Structuralist critics consider the structure of types of literature. The Harry Potter books are a part of the fantasy genre. Think about Harry Potter in relationship to the fantasy genre and other fairy tales. How is meaning created through the relationship between the Harry Potter books and other stories in this genre? How is the role of the fairy tale important in *Harry Potter and the Deathly Hallows*?

A thesis statement for a structuralist critique analyzing the role Harry Potter plays in the fantasy genre might be the following: *Harry Potter and the Deathly Hallows* includes a wizard fairy tale that ultimately foreshadows Harry's own story with Voldemort and suggests Harry's story, like all fairy tales, has a moral for the reader.

You Critique It

Now that you have learned about different critical theories and how to apply them to literature, are you ready to perform your own critique? You have read that this type of evaluation can help you look at literature in a new way and make you pay attention to certain issues you may not have otherwise recognized. So, why not use one of the critical theories profiled in this book to consider a fresh take on your favorite book?

First, choose a theory and the book you want to analyze. Remember that the theory is a springboard for asking questions about the work.

Next, write a specific question that relates to the theory you have selected. Then you can form your thesis, which should provide the answer to that question. Your thesis is the most important part of your critique and offers an argument about the work based on the tenets, or beliefs, of the theory you are applying. Recall that the thesis statement typically appears at the very end of the introductory paragraph of your essay. It is usually only one sentence long.

After you have written your thesis, find evidence to back it up. Good places to start are in the work itself or in journals or articles that discuss what other people have said about it. Since you are critiquing a book, you may also want to read about the author's life so you can get a sense of what factors may have affected the creative process. This can be especially useful if working within historical, biographical, or psychological criticism.

Depending on which theory you are applying, you can often find evidence in the book's language, plot, or character development. You should also explore parts of the book that seem to disprove your thesis and create an argument against them. As you do this, you might want to address what other critics have written about the book. Their quotes may help support your claim.

Before you start analyzing a work, think about the different arguments made in this book. Reflect on how evidence supporting the thesis was presented. Did you find that some of the techniques used to back up the arguments were more convincing than others? Try these methods as you prove your thesis in your own critique.

When you are finished writing your critique, read it over carefully. Is your thesis statement understandable? Do the supporting arguments flow logically, with the topic of each paragraph clearly stated? Can you add any information that would present your readers with a stronger argument in favor of your thesis? Were you able to use quotes from the book, as well as from other critics, to enhance your ideas?

Did you see the work in a new light?

Timeline

Rowling graduates from the University of Exeter.

1965
Joanne Rowling is born in Chipping Sodbury, England, on July 31.

2003
Harry Potter and the Order of the Phoenix is published.

Rowling and Murray's son, David, is born.

2004
The film version of Harry Potter and the Prisoner of Azkaban is released.

2005
Harry Potter and the Half-Blood Prince is published.

The film version of Harry Potter and the Goblet of Fire is released.

Rowling and Murray's daughter Mackenzie is born.

2007
Harry Potter and the Deathly Hallows is published.

The film version of Harry Potter and the Order of the Phoenix is released.

1991
Rowling moves to Porto, Portugal, to teach English.

1992
Rowling marries Jorge Arantes.

1993
Rowling and Arantes's daughter, Jessica, is born.

1995
Rowling divorces Arantes.

1997
Harry Potter and the Philosopher's Stone is published in the United Kingdom.

1998
Harry Potter and the Chamber of Secrets is published in the United Kingdom.

1999
Harry Potter and the Prisoner of Azkaban is published.

2000
Harry Potter and the Goblet of Fire is published.

2001
Rowling marries Neil Murray.

The film version of *Harry Potter and the Sorcerer's Stone* is released.

2002
The film version of *Harry Potter and the Chamber of Secrets* is released.

2009
The film version of *Harry Potter and the Half-Blood Prince* is released.

2010
The first half of the film version of *Harry Potter and the Deathly Hallows* is released.

2011
The second half of the film version of *Harry Potter and the Deathly Hallows* is released.

Glossary

binary oppositions
Word pairs that are opposites, such as love and hate.

colonialism
When one powerful nation dominates another.

communism
A system of redistributing wealth so that there is no private property and all people share all resources.

compromise formation
When the conscious mind channels an unconscious desire into a similar obsessive behavior in order to release tension regarding the unconscious desire.

corporeal
Having a physical body.

covert
Hidden.

diadem
A crown.

dyads
The two concepts that make a pair.

economic classes
Grouping people according to how much money they earn.

genre
A category of literature, music, or art grouped by style.

industrialism
> When large-scale industries have dominance.

inversion
> When the unconscious mind converts a repressed desire into an interest that is oppositional in nature.

neurotic
> Characterized by unhealthy obsessive behavior; often caused by a mental or emotional disorder.

overt
> Openly revealed.

repress
> The process of preventing the expression of particular desires.

socialized
> The process of training someone to behave in a way that is socially acceptable.

unconscious
> The part of the mind that is hidden from the conscious self.

Bibliography of Works and Criticism

Important Works

Harry Potter and the Philosopher's Stone (UK), 1997

Harry Potter and the Sorcerer's Stone (US), 1998

Harry Potter and the Chamber of Secrets (UK), 1998

Harry Potter and the Chamber of Secrets (US), 1999

Harry Potter and the Prisoner of Azkaban, 1999

Harry Potter and the Goblet of Fire, 2000

Harry Potter and the Order of the Phoenix, 2003

Harry Potter and the Half-Blood Prince, 2005

Harry Potter and the Deathly Hallows, 2007

The Tales of Beedle the Bard, 2008

Critical Discussions

Barry, Peter. *Beginning Theory: An Introduction to Literary and Cultural Theory*. New York: Manchester UP, 2002. Print.

Bryfonski, Dedria, ed. *Political Issues in J. K. Rowling's Harry Potter Series*. Detroit, MI: Greenhaven, 2009. Print.

Heilman, Elizabeth E., ed. *Harry Potter's World: Multidisciplinary Critical Perspectives*. New York: Routledge, 2003. Print.

Lynn, Steven. *Texts and Contexts: Writing about Literature with Critical Theory*. 5th ed. New York: Pearson, 2008. Print.

Rivkin, Julie, and Michael Ryan, eds. *Literary Theory: An Anthology*. 2nd ed. Malden, MA: Blackwell, 2004. Print.

Resources

Selected Bibliography

Blake, Andrew. *The Irresistible Rise of Harry Potter*. New York: Verso, 2002. Print.

Gupta, Suman. *Re-Reading Harry Potter*. New York: Palgrave, 2003. Print.

Rowling, J. K. *Harry Potter and the Deathly Hallows*. New York: Scholastic, 2007. Print.

Rowling, J. K. *Harry Potter and the Goblet of Fire*. New York: Scholastic, 2000. Print.

Rowling, J. K. *Harry Potter and the Half-Blood Prince*. New York: Scholastic, 2005. Print.

Rowling, J. K. *Harry Potter and the Sorcerer's Stone*. New York: Scholastic, 1997. Print.

Further Readings

Baggett, David, and Shawn E. Klein, eds. *Harry Potter and Philosophy: If Aristotle Ran Hogwarts*. Chicago, IL: Open Court, 2004. Print.

Beahm, George. *Muggles and Magic: J. K. Rowling and the Harry Potter Phenomenon*. 3rd ed. Charlottesville, VA: Hampton Roads, 2007. Print.

Lackey, Mercedes, ed. *Mapping the World of Harry Potter*. Dallas, TX: BenBella, 2006. Print.

Vander Ark, Steve. *The Lexicon: An Unauthorized Guide to Harry Potter Fiction and Related Materials*. Muskegon, MI: RDR Books, 2009. Print.

Web Links

To learn more about critiquing the works of J. K.
Rowling, visit ABDO Publishing Company online at
www.abdopublishing.com. Web sites about the works
of J. K. Rowling are featured on our Book Links page.
These links are routinely monitored and updated to
provide the most current information available.

For More Information
J. K. Rowling Official Web Site

www.jkrowling.com

Author J. K. Rowling's official site offers a biography,
news, and extra information about the characters found
in the Harry Potter books.

The Wizarding World of Harry Potter

Universal Studios, Orlando, Florida

407-224-4233

www.universalorlandoresort.com/harrypotter

This is the wizarding world of Harry Potter brought to
life. Visit Hogwarts Castle and Hogsmeade.

Source Notes

Chapter 1. Introduction to Critiques

None.

Chapter 2. A Closer Look at J. K. Rowling

None.

Chapter 3. An Overview of *Harry Potter and the Sorcerer's Stone*

None.

Chapter 4. How to Apply Biographical Criticism to *Harry Potter and the Sorcerer's Stone*

1. Lindsey Fraser. *Conversations with J. K. Rowling*. New York: Scholastic, 2001. Print. 20.

2. Ibid. 23.

3. George Beahm. *Muggles and Magic: J. K. Rowling and the Harry Potter Phenomenon*. 3rd ed. Charlottesville, VA: Hampton Roads, 2007. Print. 95.

Chapter 5. An Overview of *Harry Potter and the Goblet of Fire*

None.

Chapter 6. How to Apply Marxist Criticism to *Harry Potter and the Goblet of Fire*

1. Jack Zipes. *Sticks and Stones: The Troublesome Success of Children's Literature from Slovenly Peter to Harry Potter*. New York: Routledge, 2001. Print. 183.

Chapter 7. An Overview of *Harry Potter and the Half-Blood Prince*

None.

Chapter 8. How to Apply Psychoanalytic Criticism to *Harry Potter and the Half-Blood Prince*

1. J. K. Rowling. *Harry Potter and the Half-Blood Prince*. New York: Scholastic, 2005. Print. 185.

2. Ibid. 183.

3. Julie Rivkin, and Michael Ryan, eds. *Literary Theory: An Anthology*. 2nd ed. Malden, MA: Blackwell, 2004. Print. 390.

4. J. K. Rowling. *Harry Potter and the Half-Blood Prince*. New York: Scholastic, 2005. Print. 262.

5. Ibid. 275.

Chapter 9. An Overview of *Harry Potter and the Deathly Hallows*

None.

Chapter 10. How to Apply Structuralism to *Harry Potter and the Deathly Hallows*

1. Peter Barry. *Beginning Theory: An Introduction to Literary and Cultural Theory*. New York: Manchester UP, 2002. Print. 39.

Index

Index Continued

About the Author

Victoria Peterson-Hilleque is a freelance writer who lives and works in Minneapolis, Minnesota. Her book *J. K. Rowling: Extraordinary Author* was published in 2010. She has a master's degree in English literature from the University of St. Thomas in St. Paul, Minnesota, and a master's in fine arts from Hamline University, also in St. Paul.

Photo Credits

Anthony Harvey/PictureGroup/AP Images, cover, 3; Richard Lewis/AP Images, 12, 98 (top); David Cheskin/AP Images, 17; Anthony Harvey/AP Images, 18, 98 (bottom); Warner Bros./Photofest, 20, 23, 25, 28, 34, 38, 42, 46, 51, 61, 64, 69, 74, 78, 84, 90, 92; Jon Furniss/WireImage/Getty Images, 56, 99